This Book

I wish some nights lasted forever!

Hosting Tips

1. Set a specific time for your event.
2. Serve at least 3 courses including dessert.
3. Provide plenty of alcoholic and non-alcoholic beverages.
4. Prepare as much as you can in advance.
5. Set the ambience you desire.
6. Wear an apron to protect your outfit.
7. Ask someone to serve beverages for you.
8. Make sure the dishwasher is empty and also the trash.
9. Set your table ahead of time.
10. Prepare dessert ahead of time or ask a guest to bring some.
11. Pull out all of the important items you need that you don't use everyday.
12. Make a seating plan if your guests are not opposed to it.
13. Serve light appetizers to save room for the main course.
14. Add your own favorite tips below:

_____

_____

_____

_____

_____

_____

_____

_____

_____

_____

_____

_____

_____

_____

_____

_____

_____

When was our gathering:
_____

Where were we:
_____
_____

Who attended:
_____
_____
_____
_____
_____

What foods we enjoyed:
_____
_____
_____
_____
_____
_____
_____

Wines we paired ... Place labels or details below:
_____
_____
_____
_____
_____

Notes / Stories

When was our gathering:
_____

Where were we:
_____
_____

Who attended:
_____
_____
_____
_____

What foods we enjoyed:
_____
_____
_____
_____
_____
_____

Wines we paired ... Place labels or details below:
_____
_____
_____
_____
_____
_____
_____

Notes / Stories

When was our gathering:
_____

Where were we:
_____
_____

Who attended:
_____
_____
_____
_____
_____

What foods we enjoyed:
_____
_____
_____
_____
_____
_____
_____

Wines we paired ... Place labels or details below:
_____
_____
_____
_____
_____
_____

Notes / Stories

_____
_____
_____
_____
_____
_____
_____
_____
_____
_____
_____
_____
_____
_____
_____
_____
_____
_____
_____
_____
_____
_____
_____
_____
_____
_____
_____

When was our gathering:
_____

Where were we:
_____

Who attended:
_____
_____
_____
_____

What foods we enjoyed:
_____
_____
_____
_____
_____
_____

Wines we paired ... Place labels or details below:
_____
_____
_____
_____
_____
_____

Notes / Stories

When was our gathering:

_____

Where were we:

_____
_____

Who attended:

_____
_____
_____
_____
_____

What foods we enjoyed:

_____
_____
_____
_____
_____
_____
_____

Wines we paired ... Place labels or details below:

_____
_____
_____
_____
_____
_____

Notes / Stories

When was our gathering:
_____

Where were we:
_____
_____

Who attended:
_____
_____
_____
_____
_____

What foods we enjoyed:
_____
_____
_____
_____
_____
_____

Wines we paired ... Place labels or details below:
_____
_____
_____
_____
_____
_____

Notes / Stories

When was our gathering:

_____

Where were we:

_____

_____

Who attended:

_____

_____

_____

_____

What foods we enjoyed:

_____

_____

_____

_____

_____

_____

Wines we paired ... Place labels or details below:

_____

_____

_____

_____

_____

_____

Notes / Stories

_____
_____
_____
_____
_____
_____
_____
_____
_____
_____
_____
_____
_____
_____
_____
_____
_____
_____
_____
_____
_____
_____
_____
_____
_____
_____

When was our gathering:
_____

Where were we:
_____

Who attended:
_____
_____
_____
_____

What foods we enjoyed:
_____
_____
_____
_____
_____
_____

Wines we paired ... Place labels or details below:
_____
_____
_____
_____
_____
_____

Notes / Stories

When was our gathering:
_____

Where were we:
_____
_____

Who attended:
_____
_____
_____
_____

What foods we enjoyed:
_____
_____
_____
_____
_____
_____

Wines we paired ... Place labels or details below:
_____
_____
_____
_____
_____

Notes / Stories

_____

_____

_____

_____

_____

_____

_____

_____

_____

_____

_____

_____

_____

_____

_____

_____

_____

_____

_____

_____

_____

_____

_____

_____

_____

_____

_____

When was our gathering:

_____

Where were we:

_____

_____

Who attended:

_____

_____

_____

_____

_____

What foods we enjoyed:

_____

_____

_____

_____

_____

_____

_____

Wines we paired ... Place labels or details below:

_____

_____

_____

_____

_____

_____

Notes / Stories

_____
_____
_____
_____
_____
_____
_____
_____
_____
_____
_____
_____
_____
_____
_____
_____
_____
_____
_____
_____
_____
_____
_____
_____
_____
_____
_____
_____

When was our gathering:

_____

Where were we:

_____
_____

Who attended:

_____
_____
_____
_____
_____

What foods we enjoyed:

_____
_____
_____
_____
_____
_____
_____

Wines we paired ... Place labels or details below:

_____
_____
_____
_____
_____
_____

Notes / Stories

When was our gathering:
_____

Where were we:
_____

Who attended:
_____
_____
_____
_____

What foods we enjoyed:
_____
_____
_____
_____
_____
_____

Wines we paired ... Place labels or details below:
_____
_____
_____
_____
_____
_____

Notes / Stories

When was our gathering:
_____

Where were we:
_____
_____

Who attended:
_____
_____
_____
_____
_____

What foods we enjoyed:
_____
_____
_____
_____
_____
_____
_____

Wines we paired ... Place labels or details below:
_____
_____
_____
_____
_____
_____

Notes / Stories

_____
_____
_____
_____
_____
_____
_____
_____
_____
_____
_____
_____
_____
_____
_____
_____
_____
_____
_____
_____
_____
_____
_____
_____
_____
_____

When was our gathering:
_____

Where were we:
_____
_____

Who attended:
_____
_____
_____
_____
_____

What foods we enjoyed:
_____
_____
_____
_____
_____
_____
_____

Wines we paired ... Place labels or details below:
_____
_____
_____
_____
_____
_____

Notes / Stories

When was our gathering:
_____

Where were we:
_____
_____

Who attended:
_____
_____
_____
_____
_____

What foods we enjoyed:
_____
_____
_____
_____
_____
_____
_____

Wines we paired ... Place labels or details below:
_____
_____
_____
_____
_____
_____

Notes / Stories

_____
_____
_____
_____
_____
_____
_____
_____
_____
_____
_____
_____
_____
_____
_____
_____
_____
_____
_____
_____
_____
_____
_____
_____

When was our gathering:
_____

Where were we:
_____
_____

Who attended:
_____
_____
_____
_____
_____

What foods we enjoyed:
_____
_____
_____
_____
_____
_____

Wines we paired ... Place labels or details below:
_____
_____
_____
_____
_____
_____

Notes / Stories

When was our gathering:
_____

Where were we:
_____
_____

Who attended:
_____
_____
_____
_____
_____

What foods we enjoyed:
_____
_____
_____
_____
_____
_____
_____

Wines we paired ... Place labels or details below:
_____
_____
_____
_____
_____
_____
_____

Notes / Stories

_____
_____
_____
_____
_____
_____
_____
_____
_____
_____
_____
_____
_____
_____
_____
_____
_____
_____
_____
_____
_____
_____
_____
_____
_____
_____
_____

When was our gathering:

_____

Where were we:

_____

_____

Who attended:

_____

_____

_____

_____

What foods we enjoyed:

_____

_____

_____

_____

_____

_____

Wines we paired ... Place labels or details below:

_____

_____

_____

_____

_____

_____

Notes / Stories

When was our gathering:
_____

Where were we:
_____
_____

Who attended:
_____
_____
_____
_____
_____

What foods we enjoyed:
_____
_____
_____
_____
_____
_____
_____

Wines we paired ... Place labels or details below:
_____
_____
_____
_____
_____
_____
_____

Notes / Stories

When was our gathering:
_____

Where were we:
_____
_____

Who attended:
_____
_____
_____
_____
_____

What foods we enjoyed:
_____
_____
_____
_____
_____
_____

Wines we paired ... Place labels or details below:
_____
_____
_____
_____
_____
_____

Notes / Stories

_____
_____
_____
_____
_____
_____
_____
_____
_____
_____
_____
_____
_____
_____
_____
_____
_____
_____
_____
_____
_____
_____
_____
_____
_____
_____

When was our gathering:

_____

Where were we:

_____

_____

Who attended:

_____

_____

_____

_____

_____

What foods we enjoyed:

_____

_____

_____

_____

_____

_____

_____

Wines we paired ... Place labels or details below:

_____

_____

_____

_____

_____

_____

Notes / Stories

When was our gathering:
_____

Where were we:
_____
_____

Who attended:
_____
_____
_____
_____
_____

What foods we enjoyed:
_____
_____
_____
_____
_____
_____

Wines we paired ... Place labels or details below:
_____
_____
_____
_____
_____
_____

Notes / Stories

When was our gathering:

_____

Where were we:

_____

_____

Who attended:

_____

_____

_____

_____

_____

What foods we enjoyed:

_____

_____

_____

_____

_____

_____

_____

Wines we paired ... Place labels or details below:

_____

_____

_____

_____

_____

_____

Notes / Stories

When was our gathering:
_____

Where were we:
_____
_____

Who attended:
_____
_____
_____
_____
_____

What foods we enjoyed:
_____
_____
_____
_____
_____
_____

Wines we paired ... Place labels or details below:
_____
_____
_____
_____
_____
_____

Notes / Stories

_____
_____
_____
_____
_____
_____
_____
_____
_____
_____
_____
_____
_____
_____
_____
_____
_____
_____
_____
_____
_____
_____
_____
_____
_____
_____
_____
_____
_____

When was our gathering:
_____

Where were we:
_____
_____

Who attended:
_____
_____
_____
_____
_____

What foods we enjoyed:
_____
_____
_____
_____
_____
_____

Wines we paired ... Place labels or details below:
_____
_____
_____
_____
_____
_____
_____

Notes / Stories

When was our gathering:

Where were we:

Who attended:

What foods we enjoyed:

Wines we paired ... Place labels or details below:

Notes / Stories

When was our gathering:
_____

Where were we:
_____
_____

Who attended:
_____
_____
_____
_____
_____

What foods we enjoyed:
_____
_____
_____
_____
_____
_____
_____

Wines we paired ... Place labels or details below:
_____
_____
_____
_____
_____
_____
_____

Notes / Stories

_____
_____
_____
_____
_____
_____
_____
_____
_____
_____
_____
_____
_____
_____
_____
_____
_____
_____
_____
_____
_____
_____
_____
_____
_____

When was our gathering:
_____

Where were we:
_____
_____

Who attended:
_____
_____
_____
_____
_____

What foods we enjoyed:
_____
_____
_____
_____
_____
_____
_____

Wines we paired ... Place labels or details below:
_____
_____
_____
_____
_____

Notes / Stories

When was our gathering:

_____

Where were we:

_____
_____

Who attended:

_____
_____
_____
_____
_____

What foods we enjoyed:

_____
_____
_____
_____
_____
_____

Wines we paired ... Place labels or details below:

_____
_____
_____
_____
_____
_____

Notes / Stories

_____

_____

_____

_____

_____

_____

_____

_____

_____

_____

_____

_____

_____

_____

_____

_____

_____

_____

_____

_____

_____

_____

_____

_____

_____

When was our gathering:

_____

Where were we:

_____
_____

Who attended:

_____
_____
_____
_____
_____

What foods we enjoyed:

_____
_____
_____
_____
_____
_____
_____

Wines we paired ... Place labels or details below:

_____
_____
_____
_____
_____
_____

Notes / Stories

When was our gathering:
_____

Where were we:
_____
_____

Who attended:
_____
_____
_____
_____
_____

What foods we enjoyed:
_____
_____
_____
_____
_____
_____
_____

Wines we paired ... Place labels or details below:
_____
_____
_____
_____
_____
_____

Notes / Stories

When was our gathering:

_____

Where were we:

_____

Who attended:

_____
_____
_____
_____

What foods we enjoyed:

_____
_____
_____
_____
_____
_____

Wines we paired ... Place labels or details below:

_____
_____
_____
_____
_____

Notes / Stories

_____
_____
_____
_____
_____
_____
_____
_____
_____
_____
_____
_____
_____
_____
_____
_____
_____
_____
_____
_____
_____
_____
_____
_____
_____

When was our gathering:

_____

Where were we:

_____

_____

Who attended:

_____

_____

_____

_____

_____

What foods we enjoyed:

_____

_____

_____

_____

_____

_____

_____

Wines we paired ... Place labels or details below:

_____

_____

_____

_____

_____

_____

Notes / Stories

_____
_____
_____
_____
_____
_____
_____
_____
_____
_____
_____
_____
_____
_____
_____
_____
_____
_____
_____
_____
_____
_____
_____
_____
_____
_____
_____

When was our gathering:
_____

Where were we:
_____
_____

Who attended:
_____
_____
_____
_____
_____

What foods we enjoyed:
_____
_____
_____
_____
_____
_____
_____

Wines we paired ... Place labels or details below:
_____
_____
_____
_____
_____
_____
_____

Notes / Stories

_____

_____

_____

_____

_____

_____

_____

_____

_____

_____

_____

_____

_____

_____

_____

_____

_____

_____

_____

_____

_____

_____

_____

_____

_____

When was our gathering: _____

Where were we: _____
_____

Who attended: _____
_____
_____
_____
_____

What foods we enjoyed: _____
_____
_____
_____
_____
_____
_____

Wines we paired ... Place labels or details below:
_____
_____
_____
_____
_____
_____

Notes / Stories

_____

_____

_____

_____

_____

_____

_____

_____

_____

_____

_____

_____

_____

_____

_____

_____

_____

_____

_____

_____

_____

_____

_____

_____

_____

_____

When was our gathering:

_____

Where were we:

_____
_____

Who attended:

_____
_____
_____
_____
_____

What foods we enjoyed:

_____
_____
_____
_____
_____
_____

Wines we paired ... Place labels or details below:

_____
_____
_____
_____
_____
_____

Notes / Stories

When was our gathering:
_____

Where were we:
_____
_____

Who attended:
_____
_____
_____
_____
_____

What foods we enjoyed:
_____
_____
_____
_____
_____
_____
_____

Wines we paired ... Place labels or details below:
_____
_____
_____
_____
_____
_____
_____

Notes / Stories

When was our gathering:

_____

Where were we:

_____

_____

Who attended:

_____

_____

_____

_____

_____

What foods we enjoyed:

_____

_____

_____

_____

_____

_____

_____

Wines we paired ... Place labels or details below:

_____

_____

_____

_____

_____

_____

Notes / Stories

When was our gathering: _____

Where were we: _____

_____

Who attended: _____

_____

_____

_____

What foods we enjoyed: _____

_____

_____

_____

_____

_____

Wines we paired ... Place labels or details below:

_____

_____

_____

_____

_____

_____

_____

Notes / Stories

When was our gathering:
_____

Where were we:
_____
_____

Who attended:
_____
_____
_____
_____

What foods we enjoyed:
_____
_____
_____
_____
_____
_____

Wines we paired ... Place labels or details below:
_____
_____
_____
_____
_____
_____

Notes / Stories

_____
_____
_____
_____
_____
_____
_____
_____
_____
_____
_____
_____
_____
_____
_____
_____
_____
_____
_____
_____
_____
_____
_____
_____
_____
_____
_____

When was our gathering:
_____

Where were we:
_____
_____

Who attended:
_____
_____
_____
_____
_____

What foods we enjoyed:
_____
_____
_____
_____
_____
_____
_____

Wines we paired ... Place labels or details below:
_____
_____
_____
_____
_____
_____
_____

Notes / Stories

_____

_____

_____

_____

_____

_____

_____

_____

_____

_____

_____

_____

_____

_____

_____

_____

_____

_____

_____

_____

_____

_____

_____

_____

_____

When was our gathering:
_____

Where were we:
_____
_____

Who attended:
_____
_____
_____
_____
_____

What foods we enjoyed:
_____
_____
_____
_____
_____
_____
_____

Wines we paired ... Place labels or details below:
_____
_____
_____
_____
_____
_____

Notes / Stories

When was our gathering:

_____

Where were we:

_____

_____

Who attended:

_____

_____

_____

_____

What foods we enjoyed:

_____

_____

_____

_____

_____

Wines we paired ... Place labels or details below:

_____

_____

_____

_____

_____

_____

Notes / Stories

When was our gathering:
_____

Where were we:
_____
_____

Who attended:
_____
_____
_____
_____
_____

What foods we enjoyed:
_____
_____
_____
_____
_____
_____
_____

Wines we paired ... Place labels or details below:
_____
_____
_____
_____
_____
_____

Notes / Stories

_____

_____

_____

_____

_____

_____

_____

_____

_____

_____

_____

_____

_____

_____

_____

_____

_____

_____

_____

_____

_____

_____

_____

_____

_____

When was our gathering:
_____

Where were we:
_____
_____

Who attended:
_____
_____
_____
_____
_____

What foods we enjoyed:
_____
_____
_____
_____
_____
_____

Wines we paired ... Place labels or details below:
_____
_____
_____
_____
_____
_____

Notes / Stories

When was our gathering:

_____

Where were we:

_____

_____

Who attended:

_____

_____

_____

_____

_____

What foods we enjoyed:

_____

_____

_____

_____

_____

_____

_____

Wines we paired ... Place labels or details below:

_____

_____

_____

_____

_____

_____

_____

Notes / Stories

When was our gathering:

_____

Where were we:

_____
_____

Who attended:

_____
_____
_____
_____
_____

What foods we enjoyed:

_____
_____
_____
_____
_____
_____

Wines we paired ... Place labels or details below:

_____
_____
_____
_____
_____
_____

Notes / Stories

When was our gathering:
_____

Where were we:
_____
_____

Who attended:
_____
_____
_____
_____
_____

What foods we enjoyed:
_____
_____
_____
_____
_____
_____
_____

Wines we paired ... Place labels or details below:
_____
_____
_____
_____
_____

Notes / Stories

_____

_____

_____

_____

_____

_____

_____

_____

_____

_____

_____

_____

_____

_____

_____

_____

_____

_____

_____

_____

_____

_____

_____

_____

When was our gathering:

_____

Where were we:

_____

_____

Who attended:

_____

_____

_____

_____

What foods we enjoyed:

_____

_____

_____

_____

_____

_____

Wines we paired ... Place labels or details below:

_____

_____

_____

_____

_____

_____

Notes / Stories

Printed in Great Britain
by Amazon

19507771R00059